Sheep Have Lambs

by Lynn M. Stone

Animals and Their Young

Content Adviser: Terrence E. Young Jr., M.Ed., M.L.S.
Jefferson Parish (La.) Public Schools

Reading Adviser: Dr. Linda D. Labbo,
Department of Reading Education, College of Education,
The University of Georgia

COMPASS POINT BOOKS

Minneapolis, Minnesota

Compass Point Books
3722 West 50th Street, #115
Minneapolis, MN 55410

For more information about Compass Point Books, e-mail your request to:
custserv@compasspointbooks.com

Photographs ©: Lynn M. Stone

Editors: E. Russell Primm and Emily J. Dolbear
Photo Researcher: Svetlana Zhurkina
Photo Selector: Linda S. Koutris
Design: Bradfordesign, Inc.

Library of Congress Cataloging-in-Publication Data

Stone, Lynn M.
    Sheep have lambs / by Lynn Stone.
        p. cm. — (Animals and their young)
    Includes bibliographical references and index.
    Summary: Describes the appearance and behavior of lambs from birth to eight weeks.
    ISBN 0-7565-0004-4 (lib. bdg.)
        1. Lambs—Juvenile literature. [1. Sheep. 2. Animals—Infancy.] I. Title. II. Series: Stone, Lynn M. Animals
and their young.
    SF376.5 .S76 2000
    636.3'07—dc21   00-008834

Table of Contents

What Are Lambs?

A lamb is a baby sheep. A lamb's mother is called a **ewe**. A lamb's father is a **ram**. This book is about lambs born to ewes and rams on farms.

◀ This lamb lives on a farm.

How Do Lambs Arrive?

A ewe usually gives birth to one or two lambs at one time. But sometimes a ewe has three—or even four—lambs at one time!

A ewe gives birth to a lamb about five months after mating with a ram. Ewes can have lambs at any time of the year. But they usually give birth in the spring.

When it is born, a lamb has a loud cry—"baah, baah!" The lamb sounds much like its mother.

◀ This ewe has three lambs to care for.

How Do Lambs Feed?

A newborn lamb can stand up a few minutes after it is born. Right away, the lamb tries to find food. Mother's milk is food for a new lamb.

A newborn lamb wants to suck by **instinct**. Instinct makes an animal do something it hasn't been taught to do. A lamb, for example, has never been shown where or how to eat. But less than one hour after its birth, it will suck, or **nurse**, its mother's milk.

◀ Hungry lambs drink their
mother's milk.

What Do Newborn Lambs Do?

A new lamb sleeps much of the time. When it is awake, it explores its pen or watches sheep in other pens.

A sleepy lamb stays warm by lying down in the straw of its pen. Or it may lean against its mother's body. A lamb with brothers or sisters may cuddle up with them.

◀ The ewe's body helps lambs stay warm.

What Does a Lamb Look Like?

A lamb looks much like its mother. Of course, the mother sheep is much bigger than the lamb.

A lamb's body is small, but it has long thin legs. As the lamb grows older, its body size catches up to its long legs.

◀ In time, a young lamb will grow as big as its parents.

What Colors Are Lambs?

A soft, thick coat of hair called wool covers lambs. Many lambs have white wool. Wool is also called fleece.

There are more than 800 **breeds**, or kinds, of sheep. Many breeds are white, but some are black, brown, or a mix of tan colors.

◄ Lambs can be black, white, or a mix of colors.

What Do Young Lambs Do and Eat?

After a week, a lamb begins to follow its mother around. When she is moving, the lamb is moving. When the ewe rests, the lamb rests too.

When the lamb is two weeks old, the farmer puts it in a pen with other lambs. Two-week-old lambs like to nibble on solid food. The farmer gives them a special, healthy food just for lambs. It is made from soybeans. The farmer soon feeds the growing lambs with ground corn and hay.

◀ Lambs bump heads with each other in the pen.

What Happens As a Lamb Grows Older?

When a lamb is two to three months old, the farmer takes the lamb away from its mother. That stops the lamb from nursing and lets the ewe give birth to more lambs. Lambs quickly learn to eat dry food and drink water like the older sheep.

Lambs in pens live only on the food that the farmer gives them. Other lambs graze on grass in the fields.

◀ After a few months, farmers often put young lambs in the pen.

When Is a Lamb Grown Up?

When a lamb is six months old, it is nearly grown up. But it will continue to grow a little until it is about two years old.

A sheep can have lambs of its own before its first birthday. But most farmers don't let their sheep have lambs until they are at least 1½ years old.

Most sheep live about seven years. Some sheep have lived as long as thirteen years.

◀ Lambs can grow to be large animals.

Glossary

breed—one of many kinds of sheep or other animals

ewe—an adult female sheep; a mother sheep

instinct—knowing what to do without being taught; a natural behavior

nurse—to drink the milk produced by the mother

ram—an adult male sheep; a father sheep

Did You Know?

- Sheep began living with humans more than 11,000 years ago.

- There are more than 1.1 billion sheep in the world.

- The United States produces nearly 50 million pounds (22.7 million kilograms) of wool every year.

Want to Know More?

At the Library

Kalman, Bobbie. *Hooray for Sheep Farming!* New York: Crabtree Pub. Co., 1998.

Potter, Tessa. *Sheep*. Austin, Tex.: Steck-Vaughn, 1990.

On the Web

Farm Animals around the World

http://www.enchantedlearning.com/coloring/farm.shtml

For information about all kinds of farm animals and pictures to print out and color

Kids Farm: Sheep

http://www.kidsfarm.com/sheep.htm

For pictures and captions about sheep on a farm

Through the Mail

American Sheep Industry Association

6911 South Yosemite Street

Suite 200

Englewood, CO 80112-1414

For information about sheep and lambs

On the Road

County fairs are great places to meet people who raise sheep and lambs. These fairs are usually held in midsummer and late summer.

Index

About the Author

Lynn M. Stone has written hundreds of children's books and many articles on natural history for various magazines. He has photographed wildlife and domestic animals on all seven continents for such magazines as *National Geographic, Time, Ranger Rick, Natural History, Field and Stream*, and *Audubon*.

Lynn Stone earned a bachelor's degree at Aurora University in Illinois and a master's degree at Northern Illinois University. He taught in the West Aurora schools for several years before becoming a writer-photographer full-time. He lives with his wife and daughter in Batavia, Illinois.